Winner of the Fourth Annual
EX OPHIDIA PRESS PRIZE FOR POETRY
2019

Rosetta

In Praise of Karina Borowicz

The poems of *Rosetta* by Karina Borowicz are composed in a rhetoric stripped to the essential and uttered with the disquieting and insistent familiarity of a recurring dream. It is from that compression that the poems derive their strength, and it is that tonal authority that the reader ultimately trusts to navigate the poems' dark and glittering waters. The poetry here is unlike any other. Borowicz is a master of startling insight and control. *Rosetta* is a remarkable book.

> — David Sanders, author of *Compass and Clock*

Karina Borowicz's primary concern seems to be intimacy with the mystery. And with what subtle rare sumptuous precision she sings of this mystery in which we live and move and have our being. Her poems are a medicine. Some make me feel genuine awe.

> — Teddy Macker, author of *This World*

Karina Borowicz's poetry is on intimate terms with the natural world and the daily lives of people whose humble possessions often outlast their owners. Never content to paint mere surfaces, Borowicz finds in common things the emblems of an existence hidden to all but the most sensitive observer. In *Rosetta*, her gaze takes in overlooked figures and landscapes close at hand — an elderly neighbor, a decaying garden, a crumbling house — then extends to the cosmos, seeking human resonances in the most forbidding places. Movingly and without affectation, wasting neither word nor gesture, she depicts a world where comfort coexists with cruelty: news of beheadings haunt us in our beds, and wheat fields are sown with bodies that "fall like rags" from a downed airliner. She is mindful of "the saw blade / of history" but also the way old stories and songs can shape the present and perhaps even "turn the weather." This is a poet unafraid to speak with clarity and purpose to a broad audience.

> — Joshua Coben, author of *Night Chaser*

Other Books by Karina Borowicz

Proof

The Bees Are Waiting

Tomates de Septembre (selected works in French)

Rosetta

Poems by
Karina Borowicz

EX OPHIDIA PRESS
2020

Richard-Gabriel Rummonds,
editor & publisher.
James T. Jones, acquisitions editor.
Sharon Cumberland, editor.
Gregory C. Richter, editor.
Richard-Gabriel Rummonds, design & typography.
Reece Johnson, InDesign formatting.
Bradley Hutchinson, graphics consultant.
John D. Wagner, public relations & marketing.

Published by Ex Ophidia Press
220 Parfitt Way SW, No. 111
Bainbridge Island, WA 98100
exophidiapress.org

Acknowledgements are listed on page 75.
Some of the poems were published
in slightly different versions.

Borowicz, Karina
Rosetta / Karina Borowicz

Paperback ISBN 978-0-578-68956-2

For Ben

Contents

III. Habitat

IV. Volta

I. Burning Book

The Old Country

There was another country
always spoken of
with reverence.
I didn't understand
why we'd left, I didn't yet
understand the saw blade
of history. I was nourished
by nostalgia for a place
I couldn't remember.
Wasn't there a great forest,
a bison that would lap
milk from my hand?
The scrape of that secret
dark tongue.
A woodsman's cottage,
shelves lined with carved
and painted birds.
Our fireplace was where
the stories were read
from a burning book:
molten logs, lit from within.
See the shadow of a man
in there. See a terrifying
creature with wings.
See it all fall down.

Elephant

In a clearing at the edge
of the forested hillside a boulder
is crouched. A mother elephant,
and we her children.
We find her, even in hip-deep snow,
even in the muck of spring.
When the fires of autumn
light the trees, hunters' gunshots
tear through the same distance
as the war. Where I place my hand
her shale skin stays warm.
They aren't coming for us,
I keep repeating. But there are tremors
in these woods, hidden lives
beating against plain sight.

Punishing Snows

When the punishing
snows came, Mother
would stand with hands outstretched
filled with crumbs for the sparrows.
How easily she took on
a stone gaze frightened us,
but we were scared by
the slightest things. Boots
clanging in our building's stairwell.
A dog's howl cut short
in the night. Grownups
with a finger to their lips
turning out all the lights.

Sofija

Our neighbor, she of the white hair
smoothed in a French twist. She
of flowering dresses and earrings

of mute pearl. Hands gentle enough
to unwind perfumed ribbons
from sour apples, and whose wisteria

soothed each bald-headed stone
along the top of the wall.

There was something she had that I
could use now (a paring knife,
a hairpin?) —

something she knew, that steadied
her hands, I wish she had given me.
I wish I had asked.

Preserved

She made red currant jam as if
our lives depended on it. Embers
glowing in jars lined the storeroom shelf.
In winter, a bright red streak on a slice
of bread reminded me of God's huge hand
opening in the December sunset.

Animal

I grew up dreading the cruelty
in dreams. The glimpse
of evil I was forced
to take like medicine.

I'd heard stories of kids eaten
by wolves. But in my dreams
I was the wolf, hunted,
tormented by smiling men.
Their humanity was their cruelty.
It grew in dark filaments
along with their hair, it moved across
the black planets of their pupils.

A chase. And I hid
in the most unexpected place,
not under the bed or behind
the curtains, but against
the wall in plain sight,
morphing by sheer force
of will into a creature covered
with scales of wallpaper.

Eyes closed, lids papered over.
Opening them meant being given away.

Cut Hair

A woman is an animal
with a braided tail

each morning she must weave
her sorrows into her hair
and at night

she must loosen them

they must be set free

but not here
see all the woman sadness
lifeless on the floor

Shifting Wind

Listen closely enough
with the skin, the nerves
of closed eyelids: the stone walls
of my cell are breathing
in the darkness — red,
and then black,
red again — the way
hot coals breathe
in a shifting wind.

Remember music, how one sound
followed another just so.
Remember the breaking
free and galloping, the blur
of dunes on one side,
sea racing past on the other.

That was then,
my other now.

Circle

First comes the gnawing,
the small voice not quite yet
insistent. It grows
like a beet, in a red circle
around and around itself as if chasing
the root hair of a worry. All that
movement yet still in the same place.
A handful of bread would do.
Nothing comes sliced here, only in chunks
and bits, handfuls and pinches —
enough to fit the palm or the space
between three fingers. Everything
is measured by the body, even time.
A day has nothing to do
with the sun, just how long
one can repeat the same motion
before falling down.

Siberian Cherries

Snow has the eyes
of a leopard in a tree.

You describe last night's
dream with the taste
still in your mouth.
You say to me, "I was eating
Siberian cherries, one
after another." You slid
the stones into the palm
of your dream hand.

Like any creature
snow keeps the memory
of what it has touched.
Centuries from now
snow anywhere
will remember its tongue
on my face. Snow
in Uppsala.

In your dream
it was summer
and this morning there is
still that coppery ache,
the wound of cherries
in your mouth.

The leopard can sense it.
Snow is circling
in a frenzy out there.

Wheat

Earth has a memory
of everything that passes
over it, lightly — the child
buried beneath the rubble
of the bombed-out building —
or groaning with weight:
the Buk missile launcher
that has just blown three hundred
souls out of the sky.
Buk means beech tree.
Bodies fall like rags.
People in the half-deserted
farmland pause, water bucket
in hand, or carrying home
a hard loaf of bread,
to watch the rags twist
midair before landing
in the wildflowers that have taken over
the grain fields.

The Only Story

A tulip has shattered in the rain.
A slow-motion shattering over five days of showers.
Petal shards on the grass, snails
churned up on the lawn like beached amber.
This soaking pulls everything to the surface.
Last night I dreamed I carried a child
in my arms. War was the only story
he'd ever heard. Hurrying toward what I hoped
might be safety, I tightened my hand
over his bald head like a hood.

Canes

I watch the city
unwind through
the bus window.
Old women pick
their way over ice,
men pass them
in short jackets
and tall fur hats.
Wire pens are crammed
with molting cabbages.
Sleeping loaves
have fogged the one
small window
of the bread kiosk.
Not one of us
belongs here more
than another.
Buses and cabbages,
fur hats, canes
passed down
from mothers
of grandmothers
will inherit the earth.

Truce

For everyone who steps on the bus
what fear and disappointment comes on
what tenderness what memories of childhood nightmares
and family gatherings what secrets are bundled up
in our arms fallen into a shallow sleep

when the door closes the walls of the bus
surround us the walls of a fortified city

a truce exists among us
an uneasy silence
ancient silence the native realm
of strangers and dreamers

Rosetta

It's like listening
to three different songs
at once —
if you hear all
of them, you hear

none of them.
Lie in bed
thankful
for your blanket,
horrified at the latest
beheading, amazed

at the landing mission
to comet 67P
which is tearing through space

at 30,000 miles per hour.

Vaguely warm in the beat
of your own
private blood

you know that comet
is making a terrible
noise somewhere,
everywhere.

Meant to Be

The road a long ribbon
of rising dust
the roadside stand piled
with charred flatbread

who here can say
with any certainty

they weren't meant
to be somewhere else
dressed in a stranger's clothes

II. Blue Silk

Her Last Free Dive

*Natalia Molchanova of Russia, widely considered
the greatest free diver in the sport's history,
disappeared during a dive off Ibiza on August 2, 2015.*

If breath is desire, if breath

is the urge to go on

go on, go on —

        then each of my dives

        is a little suicide, a taste

        of what lies beyond

        the going on.

The beginning
is calling —

not my name
but one name, one,
only one.

Sky separated
from water, creatures
one kind from another,
rib from rib

breath from breath.

I must weigh this body down —

it's too light,

too rebellious —

and fall back into that first

undivided darkness.

Upon a time once,
once, once —

there is just once
and it is happening
all the time.

                The body held its breath once

and sinks toward the black
voice. Fish stare
along the way, lips
healed over hooks,

freckled bodies nudged
by the headlamp's beam.
Their iridescent eyes
a final plea.

                I tear off the lamp and let it fall
                toward the voice —

There.

It is swallowed.

Blue Silk

kite over a field
of poppies
see how quickly the string breaks

blue silk is a gesture
of the invisible

she wrote poems on blue silk
but it was a dress she refused to wear

in a twisted tree
scraps of blue silk

Vermeer's *Lacemaker*

She loops thread around the steel pins
with cool disinterest. The lace,

like her father's trellised roses,
grows with lush obedience.

It is secret work, obscured
by fingers that are blurred by paint.

If only one thread were left loose, she thinks,
and leans with purpose closer to the lace

revealing the T-crossed part traced in her hair.
The work stills for a moment —

for centuries — as she plants
the wildflower seed of her mistake.

Moment

I was there
at just the right time.
That is my
life, showing up
at the moment
others don't. Maybe
that moment
was meant for me
maybe it even
waited. Maybe it was
nothing but
the silk of chance
roaring
in a sudden wind.
      And I
alone
was there.

From the Deck

Perhaps it means
nothing

the constant
gesturing of the sea:

*look over here, here
I am* —

a small swell
I like to think only I

see suddenly flatten

because what was
almost there

must never break
the surface.

Tiny

The world is big
and the insect gliding
on many legs across the long
wooden plank is small.

Tininess butts its head against
everything.
My voice not even
a momentary quiver in a great
sea of silence. A torrent
of silence that is breaking
over us sweeping everything
away.

Yet there are times
I feel that my body — heart
beating, hands at work —
is a passage, an opening
the size of a needle's eye
but big enough to let it all
pass through.

Boat Building

Black water vertigo
wave of panic
that envisions all the distances
to the bottom
I trust in my boat
trust my hands
are guided rightly
over the wood
trust when drowning comes
it will be one long
alleluia down

The Visit

There are women in my family who wanted
to become nuns, but something stopped them.

Still, one lives in the mountains, a hermit
with all her cats, a wooden kneeler in the living room
where she prays for hours every day.
She paints icons of Mary and Jesus
and saints in illuminated ecstasy.
Yet the faces all resemble her sisters
and brother.

I sat at the table in her small house.
She had become afraid of everything, it seemed —
other people, her cats dying, the end of the world.

Thinner than ever, but still beautiful,
she had put lipstick on for my visit.

Sometimes I don't know why I moved
this far north, she said, old photographs
in a pile between us.

As the light lowered I prepared to leave.
The mountains were gathering night
before the sky darkened. It was the mountains,
I knew, that brought her here.

Breaking the Fast

She woke hungry
for the first time in weeks.
Cherries, bread and cheese, a broken
bar of chocolate, handfuls
of walnuts. All that time
the space inside had grown
cavernous without her knowing,
carving away, from in there,
even her skin. Nothingness, barely
held together. Even eyes, she learned,
can lose their appetite for light
and movement.

Ravenous, she watched the world
like a child — because it was there,
because she had suddenly fallen down
into it. There was so much space to fill.
Each face passing was nourishment,
despite its cast of fear or boredom.
She watched without judgment. And although
it caused her pain, she did not refuse
the returning gaze of strangers.

Sounding

I speak
then pause. The words
don't flutter up
and away but drift
down. Lift, and then land.
Meaning earth, meaning
touch, meaning shore.

But sureness has nothing
to do with it. One can't
sound out certainties — a solid bell
won't ring. Better yet
there's a crack in it,
a danger in the ringing.

Natural Histories

Slab of hardened red silt
impressed with the tiny lace of fishes
thread of bones   eyelet scales
arranged as fallen through time   pressed harder
harder   always that needling

how am I anything but silt
before the hardening   closed eyelids tender with it
threads crossing as they fall
little bone of voice   fin
of how you loved me

III. Habitat

Escape

A ship is out there
going about its slow-motion business,
neither arriving nor departing.

The lives on board invisible
as insects in winter.

A part of me with no name
wanders far from the I whose cold hands
are in her pockets,

far from the tenements and fish-packing
barracks that anchor the shore.

My true habitat: the not-here,
that maybe island
at the other end of a long gaze.

Back here, the heavy smoke
of factories climbs, hesitates,

thins itself out
until it's just sky.

Nimbostratus

More room for ghosts
in an overcast day
more whispers collage the air
composing in a minor key

less is understood
but more of it
keeps blooming in the body
the ache of peonies
and Himalayan blue poppies
loosening past ripeness
I walk under clouds of petals

past the plaster lace
of cakes in the bakery window
the drugstore poster's
fluorescent smile
lurid rolls of taffeta
in the fabric shop's glare

the hard finish
of falsehood dulled
by the tang of wet bark
and wet hair

Closer

When water
is the whole
body

like today

I tap my fingers
on yellow birch leaves,
delicate petals of corrosion
on the iron fence,
stone wings
folded against stone
shoulders

Cold rain

good rain

drive me even closer

into the phosphorescence
of lichen

The Last of Her Kind

On the hundredth anniversary
of the last passenger pigeon's death.

Martha, you are the omen
and the thing
itself come to pass and
the memory, all pricked
with the chemical-
dipped feathers
of a stuffed
with our bad intent
bird. Martha,
how little we knew
you, how much
we have forgotten:
flocks of your kind spilling
over the sky for miles
of squawk and wingbeat, guano
flung in a mirror image
on the ground,
panic and joy roiling bird
over bird farther
and farther till there's only
the black dot
of you, in a cage
on your back.

Attack

*"One-Hundred-Million-Year-Old Spider Attack
Recorded in Amber" is the headline of a* Wired.com
article that appeared on October 8, 2012.

This is what happened and keeps on
happening: the spider's raised hackles,
the on-your-back, brink-of-death throes
of the wasp. And there's the shadow, thrown
over both, of the creeping yellow stone.
We only think it's finished, but the world
moved once and keeps rolling down that path.
Someone told me that all glass — windows, this vase —
continues to pour, only so slowly we're fooled
into thinking it's solid. I want my faith shattered.
I want to feel the liquid inch along my skin.

Albatross

Driving toward
the town of my childhood
the closer I get the more
I dissolve, salt
in time's water.
Even memories
not born there
live there now. Everything
ends up magnetized
to that place — the Cathedral
of St. Basil, rebuilt
on County Street.
The shaggy hides
of mountains push
against factories.

Does it matter
that everything I'm living
is memory
that nothing happens
anymore
for the first time?

The stuffed albatross
in a glass case.
In the children's museum
I keep circling
back there. The carefully
painted backdrop: beige swath
with brown stippling for sand,
olive checkmarks
for beach grass.

And my reflection
a ghost that holds
a yellow-eyed bird
in its watery outline.

Wreck

      Planks
nailed this way
and that
bar broken windows.
Every day, I pass by
the nineteenth-century
sea captain's mansion.
Timbers giving up
the ghost of paint
to storm-cloud gray.
Weeds have taken
over and now,
late summer, are going
to seed —
spiked thistle
                and velvet fists
of mullein. Moss,
vibrant green pulsed
with russet, is eating
the roof.

      Names
are being erased
in there, linen sanded
to a greasy dust.
The collapsed rib cage
of a small whale is all
that remains of a crib.
On bright days,
the pressure of sunlight
must be excruciating
        as it crosses the floor.

And these
are the surface notes
of the deep
          humming
that will overwhelm
this place: robust
city crickets,
wasps papering
blooms on wood,
the jabber of sparrows
in the haywire rose beds.
          All the dizzying
business of abandon.

Memory

I've known light
like this before:
May morning
in another kitchen,
slanted sunlight a lemon slice
in the shadows
bleaching the floorboards.
In the yard apple blossoms
invade the constant snowfall
of memory. Freeze
and burn, the touch
of all those petals.

Habitat

Suddenly I feel the old turtle's
nostalgia for rain, for a breeze
thick with the rhythm of insects
as its forelegs paddle in slow motion
against the side of the glass tank,
the stunned expression on its pebbled face
the same it will wear
for years to come.

Clockman

for John Rives

While tinkering with the clock
he talks about the mechanism
that runs it, a tightly
coiled spring loosening
all week, hour by hour
until it needs to be wound again.

I'll find out what the matter is,
he says. Why the spring
unwinds for just a day
or two and locks up.
I wonder how he can think
in that room filled with footsteps —
some delicate as a cat's,
others empty suits of armor
marching in circles.

The parrot in the corner
shifts from claw to claw,
beak open as if to laugh.
From its perch it can't see
the huge flock of blackbirds
mobbing the backyard feeder.

Frame

With its green body
the dragonfly makes its way
in a world of poison ivy
and stagnant water
cars thunder by
on the highway anonymously
and without color
and in the small spaces of silence
between them
someone hammers
the framework of a house
into place

Egg

Inside the walls of the house
starlings have hatched
the nestlings whose thin cries
fill the bedroom at dawn.
Pulling weeds this afternoon
I found a hollow blue egg
beneath our window,
no bigger than my thumb,
one side cracked open
and hinged, like a door.

IV. Volta

September Tomatoes

for Kazimera Ivoškus

The whiskey stink of rot has settled
in the garden, and a burst of fruit flies
rises when I touch the dying tomato plants.

Still, the claws of tiny yellow blossoms
flail in the air as I pull the vines up by the roots
and toss them in the compost.

It feels cruel. Something in me isn't ready
to let go of summer so easily. To destroy
what I've carefully cultivated all these months.
Those pale flowers might still have time to fruit.

My great-grandmother sang with the girls of her village
as they pulled the flax. Songs so old
and so tied to the season that the very sound
seemed to turn the weather.

Volta

One by one the three stray geese
heading away toward Mt. Tom swerve
and are pulled into the bold V
moving toward me over the splintered
remains of the cornfield.

It's almost Christmas.
The gouged mud of the field
has frozen solid, sharp
even through boots.

What do they feel through their feathers,
up there, that's out of our reach?

For a moment I imagine my hands pierced
by all those quills.

In Its Body

The snow taps a pattern
on my skin. I always think of snow
as a living thing,

have always believed in its body,
that snow's silence is its own choosing.

The breath of snow.
Inaudible, but so is the breath of any wildness
to our ears.

This is the first day it has dared come so close
in a long time, and I'm not afraid.

Circling

A pen
between fingers.
How odd is that?
The everyday
startles me
with its baldness.

Tonight, a heron
I didn't know was there
flew up, a prehistoric blur,
from the frozen salt marsh.
No sound,
not a wingbeat.

A hand moved
over paper long ago,
forming the words
Beauty
          is energy.
That perfect circle
has no beginning,
just the discovery
of being said.

Never Never

Between the clock beats
a presence, a not quite

silence, maddening itself
against the tick

maybe it's mine

that half silence
never the right word, never

the bliss of wordlessness

Blaze

For hours I watch the flames devour
paper, twigs, and logs in my grandmother's
fireplace, the framed icon of a burning heart
on the wall beside it telling the difference
between wood and me, the frail old dog with milky eyes
curled up on his braided rug.

The smooth body of fire bares its fangs,
sinks its claws, hugs itself to the wood
till the wood is changed, deadened to ash
and falling away, emptied
of whatever holds a tree together.

The heart burns without being changed.
A purified oil, flammable but not
enflamed. A torch
that blazes behind a screen of ribs.

Sand

The two we throw
are the only shadows.
Not a tree
or blade of grass
darkens the landscape.
White hills of sand.
White sun.
The few words
sifted by our mouths
have the same
burning smell
as the pulverized rock
everywhere.
With effort
we pull every step up
out of the hungry sand.
You say, "Give me
your hand." To keep moving,
we must remember why
we keep moving.
      But I want
the coolness
of forgetting.
This why,
why, is blistering
my skin.

Hungry

There in the ragged
late-winter oak,
the darkest thing around —
a mourning dove's
black eye, blinking.
She sits still
a long time.
It's the first day
of Lent, and I want
to learn patience, how
to watch and wait,
hungry as a desert monk.

At dusk yesterday
we walked down the narrow
dirt road to the neighbors'
for dinner. The leather couch
was soft and deep,
and the heat, turned up,
reddened my hands.
He talked about hunting.
She showed us the quartz countertop.
Her glasses kept flashing back
the bright overhead light.

This morning, I walk
carefully out to the edge
of the woods over the hard snow
with a bucket of birdseed,
the dog following, splay-pawed
on the icy terrain.
Only the loud scrape
of our steps, and the birds'
sudden silence.

Wild Yeast

When I learned to make bread I was told
there's wild yeast in the air
from years of baking in this kitchen.
My dough wakened in that wildness and knew
the touch of many hands: *our daily bread.*
How many times I've said that without
really knowing. What have I ever done alone?

Catch

In silence there's a net
of voices that tightens if I try
to not listen
contracts to a high thin buzz
stretched taught on the horizon

tightens to near breaking

and then the fraying
which is more like a gathering
of fir trees in the distance

my insistences, half-remembered
prayers, dream monologues
drop, drop
like pinecones

Fruit

Screened by cedar trees
a woman is singing
in the small garden behind
the stone library
bare knees just visible
folded over the granite bench

no one who passes can know
who this voice belongs to
as it vines around
the iron framework of a song

an utterance with no future
no past only the now
of a pulsing throat

no one recognizes the words
just the ripeness of vowels
that give weight and a burst
of sweetness to what would have been
a fruitless day

The Backup Singer

A song streams
through the radio.
Audible light.
The man sings about
coming home to love,
the woman backup
pretends to agree, but is singing
about something else.
Her voice comes from
a darker, more distant
corner. Her cheekbones
and her ring-heavy gestures
glisten in the gentle static.
Listen to him
if you want.
But believe her.

Balance

A hawk has come
suddenly among us. We are in our cars,
we are listening to the news.

The traffic does not slow
for a bird perched on an overhead wire.
But something slows,

seeking balance under the shifting weight
as if another lead disc has been added to the stack.

Fingers

There's something frightening
about spring
once it becomes inevitable

the yellow fingers of perennials
pushing the brown leaves aside

so much movement suddenly
pulling me along against
my will

or maybe I've willed it all
who can remember what was agreed upon

Caw

Waking up to the crow call
of a dream does it, there's the scent
and shadow of purple, maybe the warm
savor of blood, shed feathers of happiness
on my pillow, who am I that can lie
content in the fragile dawn, nerves in the ear
purring, fingers curling and stretching
like a pianist's before the velvet curtain decides to part.

Farmer's Bees

A loud crack and then there's
that crack again. No rhythm,
no predicting the intervals
as with a machine beat.
This noise comes from a man's hand.

And as I pick the huge black fruit
from a row of blueberry bushes
across from the dairy farm,
the stunning silence between each loud burst
fills me with a cold dread
that spills with each violent start.

I imagine them shooting the cows
at the same time I tell myself
that couldn't be. But there's something ugly
in the air. Shaken, I watch the bees go about
their business, our business, legs fattened
and bright with hoards of pollen.

Original Wind

The original wind has not yet
stopped. Generations of hawks
have glided on the same gust
that pulls me now down
a busy street. This is all
I really know of history,
time's collision with my skin.

Trick

I put a few poems, unfinished,
between the pages of your book.

My words, so imperfect,
now with your imperfect words.

The autumn sun is shining
over my shoulder
onto the open page.

The way leaves
fall, simply.

The way, in this world,
if something is going
to happen
it happens.

Softly

I would rather scythe
hay than write poems.

I want to just listen
for a change, sway

with my sharp instrument
to a beat that's private.

The grass is high, the color
of unripe lemon, and it falls

softly as if the fall
comes as no surprise.

Acknowledgements

Grateful acknowledgement is made to the following journals and anthologies, where some of these poems first appeared:

American Life in Poetry: "September Tomatoes"
Blueline: "Fingers"
The Café Review: "Elephant," "Sofija," and "Punishing Snows"
Cimarron Review: "Original Wind"
Connotation Press: "From the Deck," "Sand," and "Sounding"
Constellations: "Frame"
Copper Nickel: "Closer" and "In Its Body"
Ecotone: "Animal" and "September Tomatoes"
Green Mountains Review: "Siberian Cherries"
Hanging Loose: "Catch" and "Caw"
Harpur Palate: "Farmer's Bees"
Iron Horse Literary Review: "Habitat"
Little Patuxent Review: "One-Hundred-Million-Year-Old Spider Attack Recorded in Amber" (Reprinted as "Attack" in this volume)
Natural Bridge: "Cut Hair"
New Madrid: "Egg"
Nimrod International Journal: "Rosetta" and "Vermeer's Lacemaker"
Notre Dame Review: "Circle"
Pilgrimage: "Wild Yeast"
Pleiades: "Canes"
Plume: "Albatross"
The Saint Ann's Review: "Boat Building" and "The Visit"
Salamander: "The Only Story"
Salt Hill: "Wheat"
Shenandoah: "Wreck"
So to Speak: "Breaking the Fast"
The Southern Review: "Escape"
Sou'wester: "Natural Histories"
Spillway: "The Backup Singer"
The Spoon River Poetry Review: "Her Last Free Dive"

St. Petersburg Review: "Nimbostratus"
Stories of Music: "Fruit"
Vallum: "Meant to Be"
Valparaiso Poetry Review: "The Old Country"

About the Author

Karina Borowicz is the author of *Proof* (Codhill Press, 2014) and of *The Bees Are Waiting* (Marick Press, 2012), which won the Eric Hoffer Award for Poetry and was named a Must-Read by the Massachusetts Center for the Book. A volume of her selected works in French translation, *Tomates de Septembre* (Cheyne-Éditeur), is forthcoming in 2020. Her work has appeared widely in journals, anthologies, and other media, including Ted Kooser's *American Life in Poetry* and NPR's *Writer's Almanac* and *The Slowdown*. She makes her home in the Connecticut River Valley of western Massachusetts.

This book was printed on 80-pound white Finch opaque smooth paper at Bookmobile in Minneapolis, MN. The text was set in Minion Pro, and the display was set in Gill Sans Nova Light and Gill Sans Nova Medium.